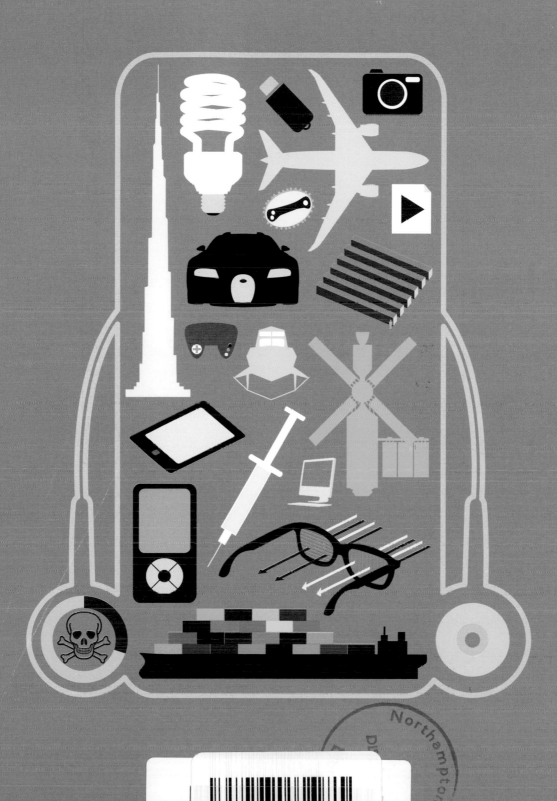

CONTENTS

WELCOME TO THE WORLD OF INFOGRAPHICS

Using icons, graphics and pictograms, infographics visualise data and information in a whole new way!

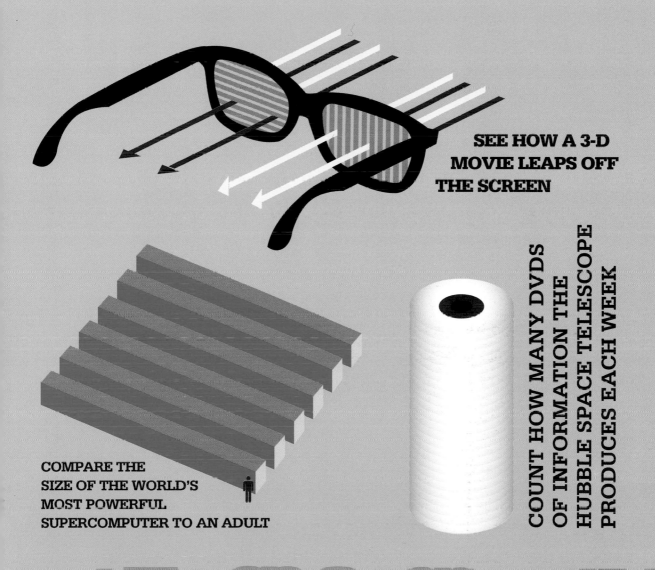

SEE HOW A 3-D MOVIE LEAPS OFF THE SCREEN

COUNT HOW MANY DVDS OF INFORMATION THE HUBBLE SPACE TELESCOPE PRODUCES EACH WEEK

COMPARE THE SIZE OF THE WORLD'S MOST POWERFUL SUPERCOMPUTER TO AN ADULT

FIND OUT HOW MANY BLUE WHALES THE WORLD'S BIGGEST STEAM TRAIN COULD PULL

COMPUTING POWER

Computer information is measured in bytes. While the earliest personal computers (PCs) could handle a few thousand bytes, today's computers can process many times this amount in the blink of an eye.

Global data traffic

An estimated **3.5 zettabytes (3,584 exabytes)** per year – enough to fill 750 billion DVDs, creating a pile long enough to stretch to the Moon and back!

Memory size

1 MEGABYTE (1 million bytes)

1 GIGABYTE

1 GIGABYTE (1,024 MB)

1 TERABYTE (1,024 GB)

1 GB = 7 mins of HDTV video

2 GB =

Information stored in **20 metres** of books on a shelf...

MOBILE GROWTH

In 2013, the number of mobile devices (smartphones and tablets) exceeded the number of desktop and laptop computers for the first time.

iPads make up **30%** of this market

2%   **10%**   **30%**

Growth in sales per year

TITAN SUPERCOMPUTER

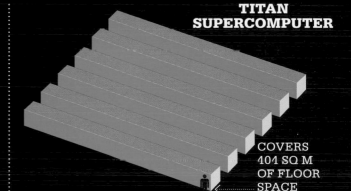

COVERS 404 SQ M OF FLOOR SPACE

Located in Tennessee, USA, it was built in 2012 by the US Energy Department for scientific research and can perform

20,000 TRILLION
calculations per second.

1 TERABYTE

1 PETABYTE (1,024 TB)

1 PETABYTE

1 EXABYTE (1,024 PB)

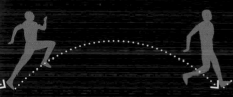

... longer than the triple jump world record (18.29 m)

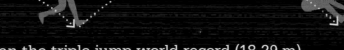

4.7GB = one standard DVD

THE INTERNET

Since its creation in 1969, the internet has grown into an amazing source of information and entertainment. The amount of data is constantly growing, so the facts on these pages are just a snapshot of the internet's development.

WHO IS ONLINE?

Percentage of internet users by continent in 2012

- NORTH AMERICA **78.6%**
- LATIN AMERICA AND CARIBBEAN **42.9%**
- EUROPE **63.2%**
- ASIA AND MIDDLE EAST **28.1%**
- AFRICA **15.6%**
- OCEANIA AND AUSTRALIA **67.6%**

78.6%
63.2%
28.1%
42.9%
67.6%

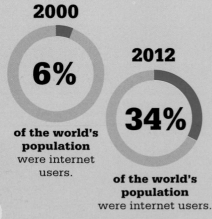

2000

6%

of the world's population were internet users.

2012

34%

of the world's population were internet users.

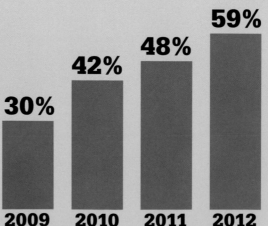

30% 2009

42% 2010

48% 2011

59% 2012

The rise of video
Bars show the percentage of internet traffic taken up by streamed videos.

INTERNET CONNECTIVITY

The growth in the number of devices connected to the internet.

● IN 2003, THERE WERE ABOUT **500 MILLION** DEVICES CONNECTED TO THE INTERNET.

BY 2010, THERE WERE **12.5 BILLION** (1.8 FOR EVERY PERSON ON THE PLANET).

BY 2015, IT IS PREDICTED THERE WILL BE **25 BILLION** (3.5 FOR EVERY PERSON ON THE PLANET).

BY 2020, IT IS PREDICTED THERE WILL BE **50 BILLION** (6.7 FOR EVERY PERSON ON THE PLANET).

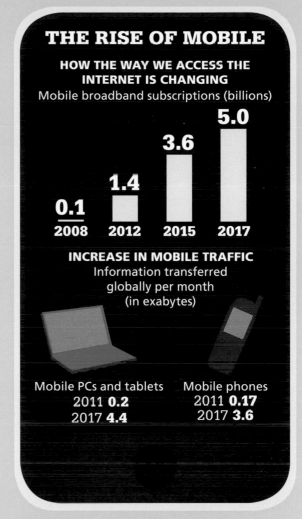

THE RISE OF MOBILE

HOW THE WAY WE ACCESS THE INTERNET IS CHANGING
Mobile broadband subscriptions (billions)

2008	2012	2015	2017
0.1	1.4	3.6	5.0

INCREASE IN MOBILE TRAFFIC
Information transferred globally per month (in exabytes)

Mobile PCs and tablets
2011 **0.2**
2017 **4.4**

Mobile phones
2011 **0.17**
2017 **3.6**

HOW PEOPLE ACCESS THE INTERNET AROUND THE WORLD:

Mobile devices now account for **12%** of global internet traffic.

This is up from **1%** in 2009.

But in **India**, they account for **52%**.

THE TELEPHONE

The invention of the telephone may have allowed people in different places to have a conversation, but modern phones have even more ways for people to communicate, including email and text messages.

THE FIRST TELEPHONE CALL

The very first telephone call was made on 10 March 1876. Alexander Graham Bell called his assistant in another room using the message

"Mr Watson! Come here! I want you."

The world's biggest working telephone was **2.47 m high**, **6.06 m long** and weighed **3.5 tonnes**. It was built in 1988 by a Dutch insurance company to celebrate its 80th anniversary.

MOBILE PLANET

How the number of mobile phones has increased since 2001.

YEAR 2001

WORLD POPULATION
6.1 BILLION

MOBILE PHONES
950 MILLION

YEAR 2005

WORLD POPULATION
6.5 BILLION

MOBILE PHONES
2.2 BILLION

YEAR 2013

WORLD POPULATION
7.15 BILLION (EST)

MOBILE PHONES
6.9 BILLION (EST)

Nokia 3310 **2000**
- **height:** 113 mm • **weight:** 133 g
- **talk time:** 4 hr 30 min • **standby** 250 hrs
- **memory:** 250 numbers • **extras:** SMS, ringtones, calculator, games

MOBILE PHONE EVOLUTION

The first mobile phones were the size of bricks and could only make calls. Modern smart phones are lightweight and come equipped with cameras, music players and more.

Apple iPhone **2007**
- **height:** 115 mm • **weight** 135 g
- **talk time:** 8 hrs • **standby** 250 hrs
- **memory:** 16 gb • **extras:** SMS, ringtones, calculator, stopwatch, games, camera, music player, touchscreen, internet browser, email, apps

Motorola Dynatac 8000X **1983**
- **height:** 300 mm • **weight:** 785 g • **talk time:** 1 hr • **standby:** 8 hrs
- **memory:** 30 numbers • **extras:** none

Nokia 2110 **1993**
- **height:** 148 mm • **weight:** 236 g
- **talk time:** 2 hr 40 min • **standby:** 30 h
- **memory:** 125 numbers • **extras:** SMS

Samsung Galaxy SIII **2012**
- **height:** 137 mm • **weight:** 133 g • **talk time:** 11 hours • **extras:** SMS, **standby** 790 hours • **memory:** 32 gb • ringtones, calculator, games, camera, music player, touchscreen, internet browser, email, apps, voice activation

The first phone call using a cellular network was made in the US on 3 April 1973 by Martin Cooper of Motorola.

TEXTING FACTS
First text sent in 1992 – "Merry Christmas"

In 2010, China sent
825,000,000,000
SMS text messages

GADGETS

The latest gadgets can hold vast entertainment libraries. A 16 GB tablet computer has enough memory for 10 movies, 4,000 songs or 32,000 photographs.

NUMBER OF IPODS SOLD

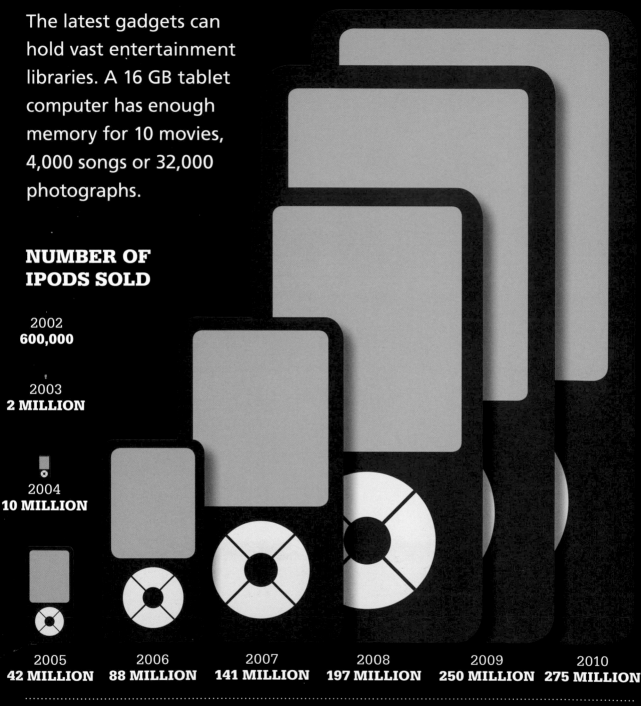

2002
600,000

2003
2 MILLION

2004
10 MILLION

2005	2006	2007	2008	2009	2010
42 MILLION	**88 MILLION**	**141 MILLION**	**197 MILLION**	**250 MILLION**	**275 MILLION**

CAPACITY OF PORTABLE MUSIC PLAYERS

1998 — 8 songs
2001 — 1,000 songs
2003 — 7,500 songs
2004 — 10,000 songs
2005 — 20,000 songs
2012

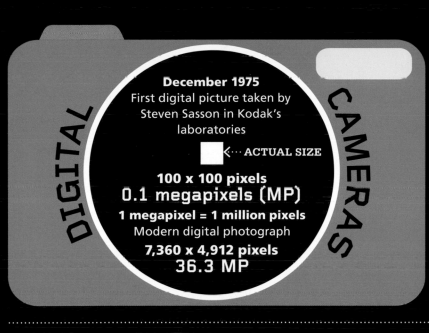

December 1975
First digital picture taken by
Steven Sasson in Kodak's
laboratories

◀··· ACTUAL SIZE

100 x 100 pixels
0.1 megapixels (MP)
1 megapixel = 1 million pixels
Modern digital photograph
7,360 x 4,912 pixels
36.3 MP

PROJECT GUTENBURG

**Numbers of books digitised by
Project Gutenburg, a scheme to
turn printed books into e-books.**

1971 – US Declaration of
Independence becomes
the first e-book

1971:
1 book

1989:
10 books

1994:
100 books

2011:
33,000 books

In May 2012, Kindle e-book sales
overtook Amazon print sales for
the first time, with

100   **114**

114 E-BOOKS
sold for every
**100 HARDBACK AND
PAPERBACK BOOKS.**

40,000 songs

ENTERTAINMENT

Technological advances have made the world's favourite forms of entertainment even more popular. The 3-D film *Avatar* became the most successful film ever in 2009, earning US$1 billion in just 17 days.

TV
DIGITAL V ANALOGUE

Analogue signals are like a wave and vary in size and shape. Digital signals are either on or off. The pattern of the ons and offs is decided by the information. Digital signals carry more information, creating a sharper, high-definition TV picture.

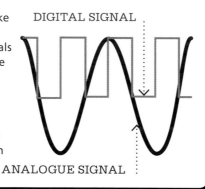

DIGITAL SIGNAL

ANALOGUE SIGNAL

STANDARD
720 X 576
pixels

High-definition televisions (HDTVs) have more pixels than standard TVs, producing clearer, sharper images.

HIGH-DEFINITION
1920 X 1080
pixels

72%
OF HOUSEHOLDS IN THE USA PLAY **COMPUTER OR VIDEO GAMES**.

VIDEO GAMES

As of January 2011, players on the online game *WORLD OF WARCRAFT* had notched a combined playing time of **5.93 MILLION YEARS!**

49%
OF HOUSEHOLDS IN THE USA **OWN A GAMES CONSOLE** (AND THOSE THAT DO OWN TWO ON AVERAGE).

HOW 3-D MOVIES WORK

3-D movies combine two images that are slightly different from each other. Special glasses only let light from one image reach each eye. Your brain then puts these two images together to produce a three-dimensional effect.

DOUBLE IMAGE ON SCREEN

THE LENS IN EACH EYEHOLE ONLY LETS LIGHT FROM ONE IMAGE THROUGH

LIGHT FROM BOTH IMAGES

LEFT EYE RECEIVES ONE IMAGE

RIGHT EYE RECEIVES ONE IMAGE

SATELLITE BROADCAST

It is possible to watch live TV images around the world using satellites. Powerful antennae beam images up to satellites orbiting hundreds of kilometres above the Earth. These then beam the images to other parts of the world.

SATELLITE

ANTENNAE

HOME

The first 3-D film shown to a paying audience was *THE POWER OF LOVE* in **1922**.

The first colour 3-D film was *HOUSE OF WAX* in **1953**, a horror movie starring Vincent Price.

44,000

The approximate number of radio stations around the world. There are even

THREE

broadcasting in

ANTARCTICA.

IN THE HOME

Time-saving appliances have been making our lives easier since the 19th century. In recent times, technology has helped to create more environmentally friendly gadgets.

SOLAR PANELS CAN BE USED TO PROVIDE 75% OF A TYPICAL HOUSEHOLD'S ANNUAL ELECTRICITY

SMALL TURBINES CAN PRODUCE NEARLY 14,000 KW/H OF ELECTRICITY A YEAR

WATER STORAGE TANK

DUAL FLUSH TOILETS CAN SAVE 26,000 L OF WATER A YEAR

RAIN WATER CAN BE COLLECTED TO WATER GARDENS

TRIPLE GLAZING CAN REDUCE THE AMOUNT OF HEAT LOST THROUGH A WINDOW BY 75%

ENERGY EFFICIENT BULBS LAST 10 TIMES LONGER THAN INCANDESCENT ONES

EFFICIENT HOMES

There are many ways of making a building more energy efficient. These range from collecting rain water and reducing water use to fitting solar panels to produce electricity.

NEW ENERGY EFFICIENT FRIDGES USE 75% LESS ENERGY THAN OLDER MODELS. OVER A YEAR, THAT AMOUNTS TO ENOUGH ENERGY TO WATCH TV FOR 300 DAYS.

GREY WATER FROM SINKS AND WASHING MACHINES CAN BE USED TO WATER PLANTS AND FLUSH TOILETS

MICROWAVES

A microwave oven causes water molecules inside food to vibrate. This heats the food.

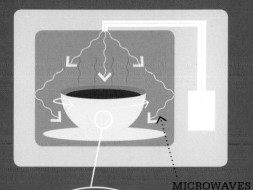

MICROWAVES

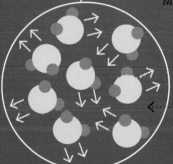

MICROWAVES CAUSE WATER MOLECULES TO VIBRATE PRODUCING HEAT

PRESERVING

Refrigerators cool food, keeping it fresh for longer. However, foodstuffs go off at different rates, so it is important to know how long each one can be kept in the fridge for.

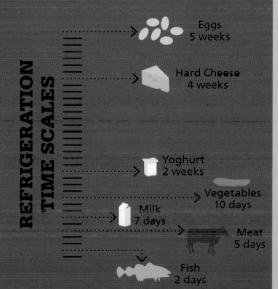

REFRIGERATION TIME SCALES

Eggs
5 weeks

Hard Cheese
4 weeks

Yoghurt
2 weeks

Vegetables
10 days

Milk
7 days

Meat
5 days

Fish
2 days

LIGHTING

Just 5% of the energy used by an incandescent light bulb is used to make light. The rest produces heat.

Energy efficient light bulbs use **90%** less energy.

If each US household replaced one incandescent bulb with an energy efficient one, it would save enough energy to light

300,000,000

homes for an entire year and eliminate

4,000,000,000 KG

of greenhouse gases – equivalent to the emissions of 80,000 cars.

SUPER STRUCTURES

Advances in technology have created skyscrapers the height of 200 double decker buses and bridges the length of more than 40 skyscrapers laid end to end.

BIGGEST BUILDING

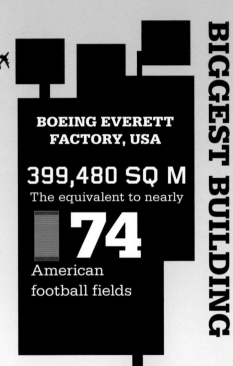

BOEING EVERETT FACTORY, USA

399,480 SQ M

The equivalent to nearly

74

American football fields

TALLEST BUILDING

To date, the tallest building is the Burj Khalifa. It is nearly twice the height of the Empire State Building, which held the record from 1931–1972.

	EMPIRE STATE BUILDING	BURJ KHALIFA
Height	443 M	829.8 M
Completed	1931	2010
Floors	102	163
Steps	1,860	2,909
Elevators	73	57
Windows	6,500	24,348
Steel (TONNES)	51,700	31,400

It took **5 years** to complete the **Burj Khalifa.**

BURJ KHALIFA DUBAI, UNITED ARAB EMIRATES

EMPIRE STATE BUILDING NEW YORK, USA

$ MOST EXPENSIVE BUILDINGS IN THE WORLD

THE PALAZZO, Las Vegas, USA **US$1.9 billion**
TAIPEI 101, Taipei, Taiwan **US$1.76 billion**
BURJ KHALIFA, Dubai, UAE **US$1.5 billion**
KYOTO STATION, Kyoto, Japan **US$1.25 billion**
BANK OF AMERICA TOWER, New York, USA **US$1 billion**

TYPES OF BRIDGE

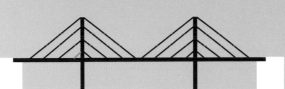

SIMPLE BEAM BRIDGE

ARCH BRIDGE

CANTILEVER BRIDGE

CABLE STAYED BRIDGE

SUSPENSION BRIDGE

The oldest bridge in the world is the **Pons Fabricus**, or Ponte dei Quattro Capi, in **Rome, Italy**. It dates back to **62 BCE.**

LONGEST BRIDGES IN THE WORLD

QUINDAO HAIWAN BRIDGE, China

42.5 KM

LAKE PONTCHARTRAIN BRIDGE, USA **38.42 KM**

MANCHAC BRIDGE, USA **36.7 KM**

HANGHZOU BAY BRIDGE, China **36 KM**

RUNYANG BRIDGE, China **35.6 KM**

LONGEST ROAD TUNNELS IN THE WORLD

LAERDAL

AURLAND

LAERDAL TUNNEL, Norway

24.51 KM

It would take just under half an hour to drive through the tunnel travelling at 50 km/h

QINLING ZHONGNANSHAN TUNNEL, China **18 km**

ST GOTTHARD TUNNEL, Switzerland **16.9 km**

ARLBERG, Austria **14 km**

THE CAR

More than 60 million cars are made every year. Advances in technology have seen cars zoom from walking pace to blistering speeds, and cross continents powered only by the Sun.

FIRST CAR

The first petrol-powered car was built by German Karl Benz in 1885–6. The Benz Patent-Motorwagen had three wheels and was powered by an internal combustion engine.

BENZ PATENT-MOTORWAGEN

1 CYLINDER, 954 CC
0.6 HP AT 250 RPM
TOP SPEED:
ABOUT 13 KM/H

BUGATTI VEYRON
(16.4 SUPER SPORT)

The fastest production car in the world is the Bugatti Veyron. A production car is one that is on sale to the public and has not been altered for racing.

16 CYLINDERS, 7,993 CC
1,183 BHP AT 6,400 RPM
0–100 KM/H IN 2.5 SECS
0–200 KM/H IN 6.7 SECS
0–300 KM/H IN 14.6 SECS
TOP SPEED 431 KM/H

A Veyron set the official speed record for a production car of **431.071 km/h on 3 July 2010**

A tennis court is **23.78 metres** long.

The Bugatti would stop from 100 km/h in **31.4 metres**.
A normal family car would need **73 metres**.

START
DARWIN

World Solar Challenge held in Australia

FINISH
ADELAIDE

...years... solar-power cars entering the annual World Solar Challenge complete a distance of **3,000 KM** in less than five days. Most cars use less power than a hair dryer, but can travel at 88 km/h.

A **1966 Volvo** set the record for having the highest mileage of any car. By December 2010, it had covered more than

4,586,630 KM

That is equivalent to driving nearly · **115** times around the globe. ·

It is still driven today and covers 160,000 km a year to car shows around the world.

VW BEETLE (22,650,000 SOLD TO DATE)

VW GOLF (27,190,000 SOLD TO DATE)

FORD F-SERIES (33,900,000 SOLD TO DATE)

TOYOTA COROLLA (ABOUT 35,000,000 SOLD TO DATE)

WORLD'S BEST-SELLING CARS

TRAINS AND BOATS

The need to carry heavier loads has seen the development of boats almost 500 m long and trains more than six times that length.

LONGEST FREIGHT TRAIN

Stretching for 7.353 km, the longest ever train was formed of eight diesel-electric locomotives, which pulled 682 cars. It was operated in 2001 by the BHP mining company and used to haul iron ore 275 km from mines to the coast in Western Australia.

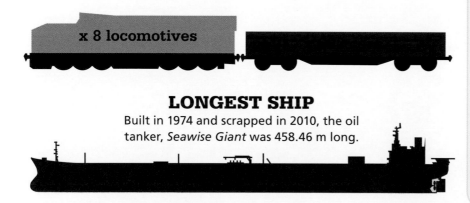

x 8 locomotives

LONGEST SHIP

Built in 1974 and scrapped in 2010, the oil tanker, *Seawise Giant* was 458.46 m long.

CONTAINER SHIPS

The latest giant container ships can carry enough containers to hold 36,000 cars, or 863 million tins of beans.

1950s 500–800 containers

2013 18,000 containers

CARRIAGE

ROLLER

WHEELS

TILTING TRAINS

Some trains travel up to 15 per cent faster by tilting their carriages as they go round corners. This allows them to maintain a higher speed.

TILT BEAM

The biggest locomotive ever was the steam powered **Union Pacific's Big Boy**, which operated from 1941–1959. It could pull a train weighing 3,500 tonnes.

HOVERCRAFT

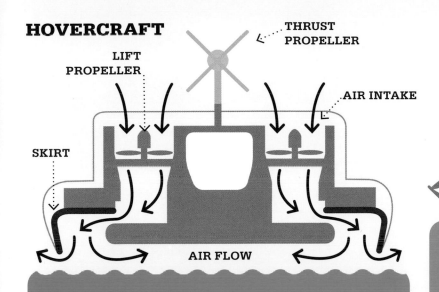

LIFT PROPELLER

THRUST PROPELLER

AIR INTAKE

SKIRT

AIR FLOW

HOVERCRAFT
A hovercraft floats on a layer of air that is pushed downwards by the lift propellers. A 'curtain' of waterproof material called the skirt helps to keep this air underneath the hovercraft. The thrust propeller then pushes the hovercraft forwards.

HYDROFOIL

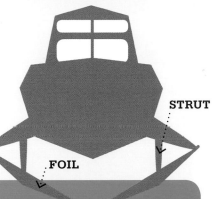

STRUT

FOIL

HYDROFOIL
As the boat moves, water flowing over the foil produces lift, which pushes the boat out of the water. This greatly reduces the amount of friction, allowing the boat's engines to push it along very quickly.

HEAVY LIFT SHIP

These ships are designed to lift up other vessels that have been damaged and cannot sail on their own. The heavy lift ship then carries the damaged vessel back to port where it can be fixed.

1 Up to 275 m long, these ships have a lowered area to hold another vessel.

2 To 'pick up' another vessel, the ship is submerged partially and sails under it.

3 The heavy lift ship then rises, lifting the other vessel out of the water.

That is the weight of nearly
20 adult blue whales.

FLIGHT

Since the first powered flight in 1903, which travelled just 37 m, planes have been developed that can travel non-stop all the way around the world – a distance of more than 42,000 km.

THE ICARUS CUP

The Icarus Cup is a competition for human-powered aircraft. In 2012, the winning plane, *Airglow*, completed the 1-km-long course in just over 2 minutes.

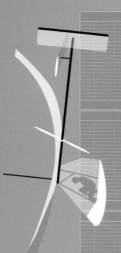

1 KM IS LONGER THAN NINE AMERICAN FOOTBALL PITCHES

SOLAR IMPULSE

The *Solar Impulse* is a solar powered plane that can fly at night by storing the Sun's energy. It holds the record for manned solar powered flight, flying for more than 26 hours, 10,000 m above Switzerland.

IT HAS 12,000 SOLAR CELLS ATTACHED TO ITS WINGS, WHICH STRETCH FOR 63.4 M

IT IS POWERED BY **FOUR ELECTRIC MOTORS**

AIRBUS A340 TO SCALE

It has completed a trip of **2,500 KM** from **Europe** to **North Africa** in three stages and there are plans to fly it around the world in just **20 DAYS** without a drop of fuel.

BOEING 787 DREAMLINER

First flown in 2009, this passenger plane's windows are **65% larger** than other aircraft. The windows use dimmers instead of shades.

To make it, workers drilled only 10,000 holes into the fuselage, rather than 1 million in a superjumbo 747.

What is a 787 made from?

50% LIGHTWEIGHT COMPOSITE MATERIALS

20% ALUMINIUM

15% TITANIUM

10% STEEL

5% OTHER MATERIALS

LONGEST NON-STOP PASSENGER FLIGHTS

SINGAPORE TO NEWARK 18 HOURS

SINGAPORE TO LOS ANGELES 18 HOURS 30 MINUTES

DALLAS-FORT WORTH TO SYDNEY 18 HOURS 30 MINUTES

JOHANNESBURG TO ATLANTA 17 HOURS

SKYLON

The proposed Skylon space plane will use a new type of engine, called SABRE. This works like a cross between a jet (in the low atmosphere) and a rocket (in the higher atmosphere) pushing it to a speed of

IT COULD CARRY SATELLITES INTO ORBIT.

MACH 25
(25 TIMES THE SPEED OF SOUND)

SPACE EXPLORATION

In order to learn more about space, we have built powerful telescopes that can peer billions of light years into space, and robot spacecraft to explore the outer reaches of the Solar System.

HUBBLE SPACE TELESCOPE

This space telescope orbits the Earth every 97 minutes at a speed of about 8 km per second. It can pass over the USA in just 10 minutes.

2.4 METRES
THE DIAMETER OF HUBBLE'S MAIN REFLECTING MIRROR – THAT IS TALLER THAN AN ADULT HUMAN.

120 GB
THE AMOUNT OF INFORMATION HUBBLE SENDS BACK TO EARTH EACH WEEK – ENOUGH TO FILL 25 DVDS.

DISTANCE TRAVELLED
These images show the total distances travelled by some of the world's most pioneering spacecraft. Some have reached the very edge of our Solar System.

APOLLO 11
THE FIRST MISSION TO LAND PEOPLE ON THE MOON IN 1969.
1.5 MILLION KM

SPUTNIK 1
THE FIRST ARTIFICIAL SATELLITE. IT WAS LAUNCHED ON 4 JANUARY 1958.
70 MILLION KM

1,400
The number of times Sputnik 1 orbited Earth in 1957 before it re-entered the atmosphere 92 days after its launch.

CASSINI
SPACE PROBE SENT TO SATURN IN 1997.
3.5 BILLION KM

1 BILLION KM

SPACECRAFT (TO SCALE)

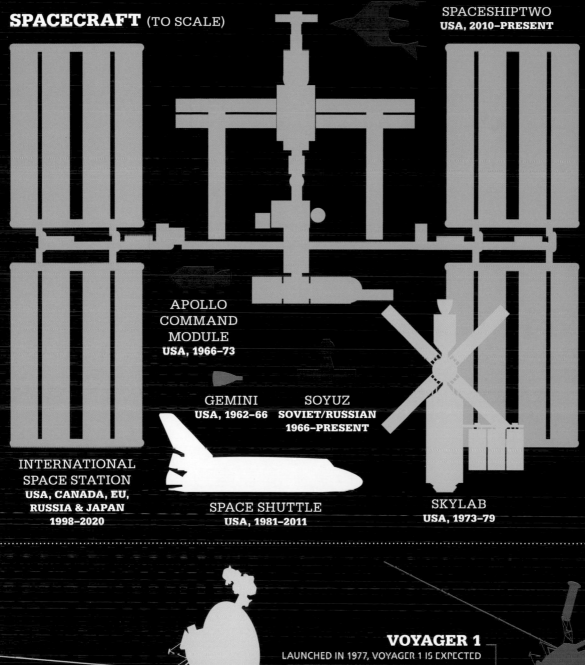

SPACESHIPTWO
USA, 2010–PRESENT

APOLLO
COMMAND
MODULE
USA, 1966–73

GEMINI
USA, 1962–66

SOYUZ
SOVIET/RUSSIAN
1966–PRESENT

INTERNATIONAL
SPACE STATION
USA, CANADA, EU,
RUSSIA & JAPAN
1998–2020

SPACE SHUTTLE
USA, 1981–2011

SKYLAB
USA, 1973–79

VOYAGER 1
LAUNCHED IN 1977, VOYAGER 1 IS EXPECTED
TO BECOME THE FIRST MAN-MADE OBJECT
TO LEAVE THE SOLAR SYSTEM.
18.4 BILLION KM

17 HOURS
The time it takes for radio
signals travelling at the
speed of light to reach
Voyager 1 from Earth.

VOYAGER 2
FLEW PAST SATURN, JUPITER,
URANUS AND NEPTUNE
AFTER ITS 1977 LAUNCH.
15 BILLION KM

11 BILLION KM

20 BILLION KM

SCIENCE

In Europe, scientists have built the world's largest machine to study the Universe. At the other extreme, microscopic structures are being developed to form Earth's strongest materials.

100°C ······> Boiling point of water

37 °C ······> Human body temperature

0°C ······>

FRANCE

LHC

SWITZERLAND

LARGE HADRON COLLIDER

The Large Hadron Collider (LHC) is an enormous circular tunnel where tiny particles are sent crashing into each other at close to the speed of light. Scientists study the results of these collisions to learn more about how the Universe was formed and how it works.

-89.2 °C
Lowest recorded temperature on Earth ········>

THE LHC TUNNEL IS **8.5 KM IN DIAMETER**

MANHATTAN, NEW YORK, USA 21.5 KM LONG

Protons race around the tunnel **11,245 times a second**

600 million collisions occur in the tunnel each second, generating temperatures **100,000** times hotter than the core of **the Sun.**

-210 °C
Melting point of Nitrogen

The LHC uses **9,300 magnets** cooled to **-193°C** using **10,080 tonnes of liquid nitrogen.** The magnets are then cooled further to

-271.3°C

by liquid helium.·····

-273.15 °C
Absolute zero

Each year, the Large Hadron Collider produces enough data to fill **180,000 DVDs.**

ROBOTS

The world's first production-line robot appeared in 1961. Called Unimate, it worked in a car factory where it moved and stacked red-hot metal parts.

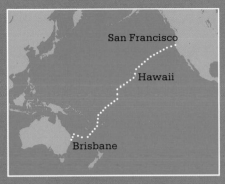

San Francisco

Hawaii

Brisbane

In **December 2012**, a self-controlled robot completed a record-breaking **16,668 km** trip across the Pacific, from San Francisco to Australia.

NANOTECHNOLOGY

Nanotechnology deals with objects that are one billionth of a metre in size. Tiny nanotubes are used to produce lightweight but strong materials, including tiny electrical components.

If a nanometre was blown up 10 million times, it would still only be the size of a **marble**, while a football increased by the same amount would be the size of the Moon.

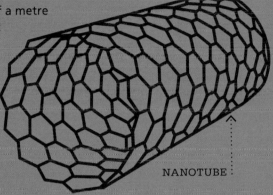

NANOTUBE

EARTH SCIENCES

Scientists use the Moment Magnitude Scale to measure earthquakes. This graph shows how many earthquakes occur each year, their magnitude and their power.

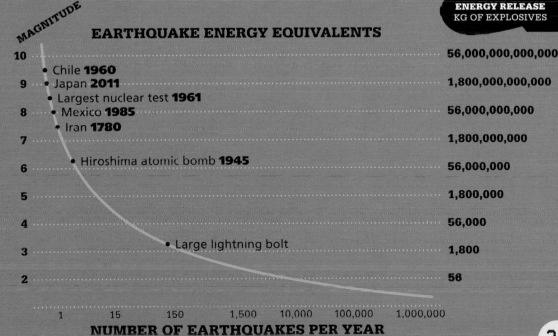

EARTHQUAKE ENERGY EQUIVALENTS

ENERGY RELEASE
KG OF EXPLOSIVES

MAGNITUDE

MAGNITUDE		ENERGY RELEASE
10		56,000,000,000,000
9	Chile **1960** · Japan **2011** · Largest nuclear test **1961**	1,800,000,000,000
8	Mexico **1985** · Iran **1780**	56,000,000,000
7		1,800,000,000
6	Hiroshima atomic bomb **1945**	56,000,000
5		1,800,000
4		56,000
3	Large lightning bolt	1,800
2		56

1   15   150   1,500   10,000   100,000   1,000,000

NUMBER OF EARTHQUAKES PER YEAR

MEDICINE AND HEALTH CARE

There are around 134 million births every year, compared to just 56 million deaths. And thanks to medical advances, many people are living longer than ever before, making the world's population grow very fast.

LONGER LIVES

Over the last 60 years, improvements in diet, health and medicine around the world have seen the average life expectancy rise.

Average worldwide life expectancy

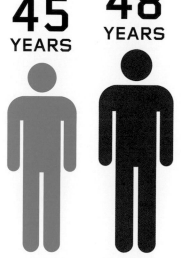

45 YEARS

48 YEARS

65 YEARS

70 YEARS

men   women

1950

men   women

2010

GUATEMALA

The influenza pandemic of **1918–1919** killed more than **15 million people** around the world - more than the entire population of **Guatemala.**

Nearly **9 million children** under **5 years of age**, or 1.4 per cent of the world's under-5 population, die each year from conditions that could be treated with medicines.

SMALLPOX

Smallpox was a disease that once killed around 4 million people a year worldwide. In 1979, it was the first disease to be wiped out by vaccines.

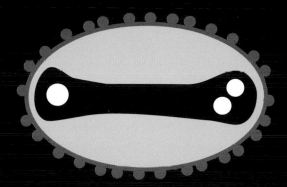

The disease was caused by a tiny virus, just 400 nanometres across – shown here 400 million times its actual size

 Smallpox historically killed

30%
of the people who caught it.

18th century
60,000,000
PEOPLE DIED FROM SMALLPOX IN EUROPE.

20th century
300,000,000
people killed by smallpox around the world.

 The last known case of smallpox occurred in **Somalia in 1977.**

TODAY, IT NO LONGER EXISTS NATURALLY.

DIPTHERIA RATES IN THE UK
Before and after use of **vaccine**

1940–1944
1,830

1969
0

VACCINATION
A weak form of the disease germ is injected into the body.

The body makes antibodies that fight the germ.

Should the real disease germs ever attack the body, the antibodies will return and destroy them.

GLOSSARY

absolute zero
The coldest possible temperature, -273.15°C, at which point molecules stop moving completely.

biennial
Happening every two years – an event that happens twice a year is biannual.

byte
A unit of computer information made up of 8 bits. There are 1,024 bytes in a kilobyte, 1,024 kilobytes in a megabyte, 1,024 megabytes in a gigabyte and 1,024 gigabytes in a terabyte.

cellular network
A set of radio transmitters and receivers used to send information, such as telephone calls. The network is divided into units called cells, each of which has its own antenna.

diptheria
A disease spread by bacteria that causes coughing and breathing difficulties. It also causes death in around 10 per cent of sufferers.

dual-flush toilet
A toilet that has two types of flush: a small flush for liquid waste; and a large flush for solid waste.

emissions
Gases and chemicals that are produced by motor vehicle engines, factories and power plants. These emissions are expelled into the air through exhausts and chimneys.

energy-saving light bulb
A type of light bulb that uses just 10 per cent of the energy and lasts 10 times longer than an incandescent light bulb.

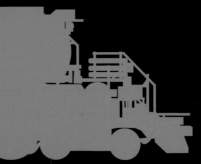

locomotive
The railway vehicle that provides power for the whole train and pulls (or pushes) the other vehicles containing the cargo or passengers.

friction

The force that occurs when two objects rub against one another. The smoother and lighter the objects are, the less friction there is.

greenhouse gases

Gases such as carbon dioxide and methane that trap the Sun's energy in the Earth's atmosphere and heat it up. This is similar to how the glass of a greenhouse traps the heat within.

internal combustion engine

The engines that power cars and other types of motor vehicle. They work by setting fire to (combusting) small amounts of fuel, causing gases to expand, which drive the pistons in the engine, which turn the wheels.

jet

A type of engine that sucks in air and burns fuel to create a powerful jet of hot gases that roars out of the back of the engine, pushing the jet forwards.

pixel

Short for 'picture elements', pixels are the dots that make up images on computer screens.

rocket

A type of engine that carries both fuel and oxygen in solid or liquid form. These are mixed and burned to produce hot gases that push the rocket forwards.

satellite

A spacecraft launched into orbit around the Earth.

solar panel

A panel that converts light energy from the Sun into electricity.

turbine

A large bladed wheel that is sent spinning as water or wind moves past it.

vaccine

A medicine given to a patient to give them immunity against a disease.

virus

A type of organism that can cause diseases.

incandescent light bulb

A type of brightly shining electric light bulb.

Websites

MORE INFO:
www.sciencemuseum.org.uk/onlinestuff.aspx
The online science section of the UK's Science Museum with games, challenges, blogs, videos and plenty of other resources for kids.

www.sciencenewsforkids.org
Information on the latest technological breakthroughs, and lots of games and facts about the world of science.

www.sciencekids.co.nz/technology.html
Free games, experiments, projects, quizzes, facts, videos and worksheets for kids of all ages.

MORE GRAPHICS:
www.visualinformation.info
A website that contains a whole host of infographic material on subjects as diverse as natural history, science, sport and computer games.

www.coolinfographics.com
A collection of infographics and data visualisations from other online resources, magazines and newspapers.

www.dailyinfographic.com
A comprehensive collection of infographics on an enormous range of topics that is updated every single day!

INDEX

ACKNOWLEDGEMENTS

Published in paperback in 2014 by Wayland

Copyright © Wayland 2014

Wayland
338 Euston Road
London NW1 3BH

Wayland Australia
Level 17/207 Kent Street
Sydney NSW 2000

All rights reserved.
Senior editor: Julia Adams

Produced by Tall Tree Ltd
Editors: Jon Richards and Joe Fullman
Designer: Ed Simkins
Consultant: Penny Johnson

Dewey classification: 600

ISBN: 9780750283076
Printed in Malaysia

10 9 8 7 6 5 4 3 2 1

Wayland is a division of Hachette
Children's Books, an Hachette UK company.
www.hachette.co.uk

The website addresses (URLs) included in this
book were valid at the time of going to press.
However, because of the nature of the Internet,
it is possible that some addresses may have
changed, or sites may have changed or closed
down, since publication. While the author and
Publisher regret any inconvenience this may
cause the readers, no responsibility for any such
changes can be accepted by either the author
or the Publisher.